ARE YOU MY PERFECT PARTNER?
To Marry or Not to Marry…

The Secrets of Happy Relationships Series

DR. LAURIE WEISS

Empowerment Systems Books

Are You My Perfect Partner?
To Marry or Not to Marry…
The Secrets of Happy Relationships Series
Dr. Laurie Weiss

© 2019 Laurie Weiss

All rights reserved. No part of this book may be reproduced in any form or by any electronic or mechanical means, including information storage and retrieval systems, without permission in writing from the publisher, except by a reviewer who may quote brief passages in a review.

The author has done her best to present accurate and up-to-date information in this book, but she cannot guarantee that the information is correct or will suit your particular situation.

This book is sold with the understanding that the publisher and the author are not engaged in rendering any legal, medical or any other professional services. If expert assistance is required, the services of a competent professional should be sought.

First published as How to Marry Mr. Right

Library of Congress Control Number: 2018909930
Paperback 978-1-949400-06-9
Ebook 978-1-949400-07-6
Downloadable audio file 978-1-949400-08-3

Books may be purchased in quantity by contacting the publisher directly at:
Empowerment Systems Books
506 West Davies Way
Littleton, CO 80120 USA
Phone 303.794.5379
LaurieWeiss@EmpowermentSystems.com
www.EmpowermentSystems.com

Cover: Nick Zelinger, www.NZGraphics.com
Interior Design: Istvan Szabo, Ifj.
Family & Relationships / Marriage & Long-Term Relationships / Self-Help

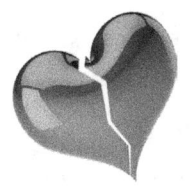

Special Bonus

For Worriers Who Want to Quit…

Finally: A New, Surprisingly Simple Way to Banish Unnecessary Worry

"Secrets of Reducing Unnecessary Worry: A 7-Day Challenge" Lets You

- Avoid agonizing over what to do
- Escape panic about things that are not likely to happen

- Save yourself from catastrophizing
- ... and much, MUCH More!

The Amazing "Secrets of Reducing Unnecessary Worry: A 7-Day Challenge" Includes:

- 7-Day Challenge
- Daily email reminders
- 5-minute daily action steps

And, I will even revealt the 3 tested magic sentences that dissolve worry.

And best of all, you'll start seeing results in less than 10 minutes a day!

Get started here and use this program to help you with the challenges you face now.

http://www.LaurieWeiss.com/Challenge

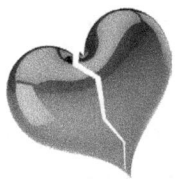

Contents

Special Bonus 3
Introduction 7
Chapter 1: Is Getting Married a Need? "I Feel a Strange Need to Be Married!" 10
Chapter 2: Not Getting Married: Is it Normal to Be in a Four-year-long Relationship and Not Be Worried About Marriage? 14
Chapter 3: A Teenage Girl Is Concerned 18
Chapter 4: What Is it Like to Be Married? 21
Chapter 5: Marriage or Amazing Career: How Can I Choose? 24
Chapter 6: Should We Live Together First or Marry So We Can Live Together? 28
Chapter 7: Should Teenagers Be Getting Engaged and Married? Three Myths That Prevent Successful Teen Marriages 31
Chapter 8: How Can You Tell If Your Boyfriend Is Ready to Settle Down And Get Married? 35
Chapter 9: At What Age Should I Get Married? 38
Chapter 10: Should I Cancel This Wedding? 43
Chapter 11: Is a 9-Year Age Difference a Problem? 48
Chapter 12: My Fiancé loves World of Warcraft 51
Chapter 13: My Fiancé Cheated on An Old Girlfriend! Should I Be Getting Married? 54

Chapter 14: My Fiancé Doesn't Stick Up for Me with My Mother-In-Law. Should I Be Getting Married?............................ 57

Chapter 15: Is He Really Ready to Commit?........................ 60

Chapter 16: Are You My Perfect Partner?............................ 63

Chapter 17: Afraid to Talk About Getting Married 67

Chapter 18: Will Dad Approve of Her Marriage?................ 72

Chapter 19: Everything Changed: These Newlyweds Are in Trouble!.. 78

Claim Your Special Bonus Now... 82

Please Help Me Reach New Readers..................................... 84

Acknowledgments 87

About the Author.. 89

How to Work with Dr. Laurie 92

About the Secrets of Happy Relationships Series............... 96

Books in the Secrets of Happy Relationships Series........... 99

Other Books by Laurie Weiss 101

Being Married... 103

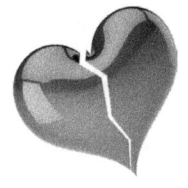

Introduction

If you are struggling with any of these very important life challenges:

Am I really ready to get married?

- Is this the right time for me to get married?
- Do I really even want to get married?
- And, of course,
- Is this right person for me to marry?

Then the questions and answers in this book will help you make the right decisions for yourself.

I've been publishing answers to questions about relationships since 1972. They've been written in lots of different formats. Here are some of the most common ones about the theme of committing to a relationship by getting married.

These are the questions of teens and twenty-somethings who are marrying for the first time. Other books in the, Secrets of Happy Relationships Series address other issues that couples experience throughout their relationships.

Here you'll find my answers to questions that include

- What is it like to be married?
- Should we live together first?
- Should I be getting married if my fiancé once cheated?
- Is a big age difference a problem?
- Is he really ready to commit?
- Are you my perfect partner?
- … and MUCH more!

Are You My Perfect Partner?

So, if you're serious about wanting to marry the right man for the right reasons, then you are in the right place! This book will show you how YOU can make the most important choice of your life — Today!

Laurie Weiss

P.S. *Are You My Perfect Partner?* Was written after I researched and wrote *Being Married: Secrets Women Wish They Knew*, the next book in this series. I refer to my research in many places as I comment on questions that I have often encountered in my practice and my reading.

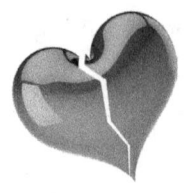

Chapter 1: Is Getting Married a Need? "I Feel a Strange Need to Be Married!"

I don't think we are all programmed to get married but it definitely sounds like Missy is. As she approached her 22nd birthday she wondered half-seriously if the strange obsessive thoughts of going out and finding a serious relationship meant she was going crazy. After being so occupied with studying and working she felt ridiculous but kept wondering if she really should focus her energy on finding a man to marry.

Are You My Perfect Partner?

There are several different ways to get programmed to be married.

- The first is biological. Your selfish genes program you with an urge to reproduce.
- The second is cultural. You are surrounded with images of married couples. Even the US tax law favors marriage.
- The third is family. If you grow up in a family where your parents are married, you expect to be married too.
- The fourth is individual. If your mother, your sisters, your cousins and your friends all got married by the time they were 25 you'll feel that you should too.

However, if you get married just because of your programming, you're likely to regret it later.

In a recently completed unscientific research project in which about 70 women answered my question, "What do you wish you had known before you got married?" many of them wished they had waited instead of responding to their own impulses. Several of them even had second thoughts before the ceremony took place and wished that they had backed out at the last minute.

So, Missy is not going crazy. She's experiencing the results of her own programming to make a major decision before she's ready to do so. She isn't the only one: it's a common problem. The signals are definitely a good way to call her attention to the question of whether she wants to get married, under what conditions and when. This would be a good time to start looking at what she wants to do with her life and even to start exploring relationships.

When she does that her obsessive thoughts may diminish pretty quickly. If they continue to bother her there are many new energy therapy techniques such as Emotional Freedom Technique and Logosynthesis that can help to eradicate those distracting thoughts.

You'll find the organized results of my research project in the next book in this series, *Being Married: Secrets Women*

Are You My Perfect Partner?

Wish They Knew. If you are really interested in what women really think about getting and staying married get your copy now.

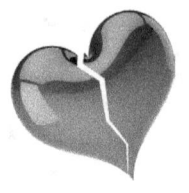

Chapter 2: Not Getting Married: Is it Normal to Be in a Four-year-long Relationship and Not Be Worried About Marriage?

(includes some interesting but dry statistics—
it's okay skip them)

If normal means that you're doing something that lots of other people in their 20s are doing, then it definitely normal to be in a long-term relationship and not think about getting married.

Are You My Perfect Partner?

The Bureau of Labor Statistics reported in 2014 that slightly fewer than half of US adults over age 16 are currently married. The US Census Bureau estimates the average age of first-time brides in 2017 was 27.4 years. For first time grooms its 29.5 Some other recent statistics show:

- The mothers of 53% of all children born to women under 30 are unmarried (New York Times).
- In 2016 unmarried households were 47.6% of all U.S. households (U.S. Census Bureau 2016).
- Only 16% of the adults aged 18-29 are married. (U.S. Census Bureau 2016).

What isn't clear is the reason you're not at all worried about marriage. It might be that you understand that marriage involves a lot of hard work. If so, you are more aware than many of the women who responded to my recent survey about what they wished they had known before they were married. Many of them were surprised by the work involved. You may be thinking why bother with all that work when we're happy the way we are.

On the other hand, you may see marriage is a very serious commitment that you're not yet ready to undertake. Chances are that you have very little idea of the kinds of benefits that are available when you make a commitment to do the work involved. Some of the women who responded to my survey reported that the rewards of doing the work were well worth the effort involved.

There are other marriage benefits that most cohabiting couples never consider. These may include a better financial situation, not only because of shared living expenses and breaks like shared insurance costs and mortgages with lower rates but because being married often involves a clearer commitment to shared financial goals.

Married people live longer and report being happier than unmarried people. Their mental health is better with less depression, distress and alcohol abuse. There's also less violence reported among married than unmarried couples. And married people report more sexual satisfaction than either single or cohabiting individuals.

Are You My Perfect Partner?

A very real benefit of commitment to working through a relationship with another person instead of always thinking you can leave it doesn't work out is that you learn and grow together. You come to depend on each other and the challenges you share deepen your sense of intimacy and connection to each other.

You don't have to be worried about marriage now in order to reap those benefits in the future when you're ready to make the kind of commitment that leads to a mature and stable marriage.

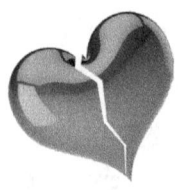

Chapter 3: A Teenage Girl Is Concerned

A mom wants to know if it's normal that her 17-year-old daughter wants to get married someday but is very worried that she will never find a man who wants to marry her. The mom reports that telling her daughter that there was plenty of time didn't seem to help and her daughter is still distressed.

My hunch is that at least two important things need to be addressed here. First is the issue of self-esteem. This young woman obviously feels that she doesn't measure up in some way. Second, it's certainly normal for a teenager to worry about attracting boys. In fact, sometimes it seems that teens think of little else. If she has not yet had boyfriends, she may be comparing herself to those girls who have and feeling that she will never be chosen.

Thoughtful teenagers may be suddenly realizing that they will be independent soon and feel very inadequate about moving into adulthood. This 17-year-old may have low self-confidence and be worried about her abilities in many areas. Talking to her mom about her worries about finding a man is an invitation to have a deeper conversation about all her concerns about developing self-esteem—not just about getting married.

Reassurance is probably useless. It is much easier to just say everything will be OK than to ask uncomfortable questions and take the time to listen to the answers to those questions. Ask why she thinks no man would want to marry her. Does she think something is wrong with her? What might it be? Where did she get that belief from? Did someone tell her? Where does she turn for information about men? About marriage?

When listening to her answers it's important to notice if she is missing important information about how to do something. There are many skills that we forget we once had to learn. There are areas ranging from basic etiquette to health concerns to cooking to money management that may be deep mysteries to some teenagers. Helping a young person identify and find a way to fill these holes can be helpful.

A life coach or a counselor can also help a young person sort through the challenges of low self-esteem and becoming an adult. If this concerned mom doesn't have the listening skills, she needs to help her daughter, or if other problems turn up, getting professional help would be useful.

If the 17-year-old is still focused on getting married, then reading *Being Married: Secrets Women Wish They Knew* would give her useful information.

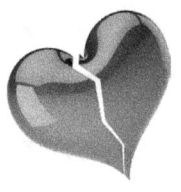

Chapter 4:
What Is it Like to Be Married?

This young woman plans to eventually marry her boyfriend and "just" wants to know about some of the reasons for divorce as well as some of the positive things about being married. This is a marvelous question because I think it is something every prospective bride secretly worries about and few risk asking.

Many of the women who answered my question, "What do you wish you had known before you were married?" were quite surprised by what it was like to be married. These are some of the problems they discovered. They thought marriage would be easy and it wasn't. They thought his behavior would improve once they were married and it didn't. They thought families didn't matter much, but they did.

Some of the positive things they reported were discovering strengths and abilities to face challenges they did not suspect about themselves and their husbands. They developed empathy and enjoyed incredible closeness and support. They reported that it wasn't easy, but it was worth the effort involved.

Your own attitude when you marry also makes a big difference to your experience of being married. When you marry Prince Charming expecting to be treated like a princess forever and then discover he is only human, leaves his dirty socks under the bed and you feel betrayed, you may be tempted to search for a better Prince. When you marry with the idea that you can always divorce if it doesn't work out you are less likely to hang in even on the days you don't like your husband at all.

On the other hand, if you marry with the idea that you will be with this man for life, no matter what, you may become helpless and resigned to intolerable conditions. None of these attitudes will help you manage the inevitable challenges you will face.

It helps to have the attitude that marriage is an adventure. As one wise friend put it, "It's like taking an unknown path through an unknown forest to an unknown destination." It also helps to have some idea of what you would like to create together. That means taking the time to each clarify your vision of what you want your life together to be like.

A commitment to creating that vision together will give you a good starting point for your adventure and help you make important choices along the way.

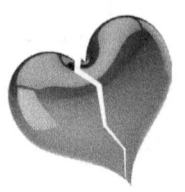

Chapter 5: Marriage or Amazing Career: How Can I Choose?

This 20-year-old college junior is struggling to resolve a dilemma. She has a vision of leaving her small-town to have "an amazing" career in a big city and see the world, but she fears that not marrying her boyfriend now will mean missing out on the rewards of having a loving husband and family. She asks, "What do you think is best in the long run?"

Tricia also gives some important background information that makes it easy to answer her question based on what I learned when I asked this question: "What do you wish you had known before you got married?" many women told me "I wish I had known more about myself," and "I wish I had waited." She is in danger of doing what she thinks she supposed to do and regretting it later.

However, it's very important for women to take responsibility for making their own decisions. Instead of telling her what to do, I would point out that she's already given me the important information that she can use to decide what would be best in the long run.

Tricia has already told me:

1. She is ambitious and has a plan for her life. She says, "Growing up in a small town I've always wanted to get out state." And, "I want to see the world and truly make some sort of difference."
2. She is being pressured by her boyfriend of one and a half years who wants to stay in this small town, close to their families.

3. She's feeling social pressure to get married now because that's what her friends are most concerned about.
4. She knows she's not ready. "I do want that [marriage and family] eventually but there's so much else I want to do. I just don't think I would be content living in a small town my whole life and as a mom."

What I suspect is that what she is actually afraid of is that this will be her only chance to marry someone she loves. She's also afraid of disapproval; the disapproval of her parents, her boyfriend's parents and her friends. She knows that she doesn't fit their world very well now but so far, that's her secret. Nobody else knows and she's afraid of what will happen if they find out.

My advice for Tricia and for many other young women who can't see beyond their immediate options is to slow down and imagine other possibilities. Think about what might happen a few years down the road if you follow your dreams and what might happen if you cave in now and do what other people expect you to do.

For starters you could imagine yourself five years from now at the ripe old age of 25. Imagine the result each possibility. First imagine marrying your boyfriend and staying in your small town. Where might you be living? What might you be doing? What is the best possible outcome in that situation? What is the worst? How would you feel about both the best and the worst outcomes—sad, mad, glad or scared?

Then imagine pursuing the other things you have always wanted to do. Answer the same questions. Next think about what you need to do, starting now, to make the best possible outcome likely to occur in each situation. Finally decide whether you are ready, willing and able to do what it takes to be happy in either situation.

Then read some of the other books in this series before you make your final decision.

Chapter 6: Should We Live Together First or Marry So We Can Live Together?

Madison's dilemma is that her parents think she should wait to get married until she graduates from college and they disapprove of couples living together before marriage. She and her fiancé will be completing their final year of college at the same school. For "practical reasons," when they are finally in the same city, she doesn't want to set up two sets of temporary living arrangements.

She wonders, "Do we live together for the few months before the wedding, but I haven't graduated yet or should we just get married early?" Madison is clearly trying to figure out a way to keep her parents happy and still do what she wants to do herself. There doesn't seem to be a way to satisfy everybody.

She has the added complication of wanting to get married in December. She's worried about which December—the one before or the one after she graduates.

To put it bluntly, she knows that in order to please her parents she should go through the inconvenience of living separately for a few months. She doesn't want to do that, so she needs to figure out which option will upset her parents the least. She also doesn't want to take responsibility for making a choice that will upset her parents.

It's clear that she and her fiancé will be spending a great deal of time together, no matter what their official living arrangements are. Then the question becomes whether to avoid the truth and practice "don't ask don't tell" with her parents or to simply make a choice and hope her parents forgive her in the future.

I would encourage Madison to test the waters by talking this over with her parents. They may be more flexible when she thinks they are. I'll bet she has never asked them the reasons they want her to wait to marry until after graduation.

If they're open to such a discussion Madison will need to think about whether their reasons make sense to her. She could also take the opportunity to share the reasons she wants to do things differently and hear their responses to her points.

In a case like this, it's best to look at the possible long-term repercussions of her decision. Research shows that committed couples who live together before they marry have the same odds of being happy as those who wait to live together until after the wedding. So, the real long-term problem is that their future relationship with her parents.

Discussing the issues thoughtfully now could go a long way toward creating a comfortable, mature connection with her parents both now and in the future.

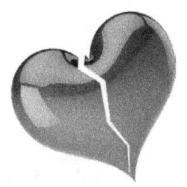

Chapter 7:
Should Teenagers Be Getting Engaged and Married? Three Myths That Prevent Successful Teen Marriages

The big problem with teenagers getting engaged and getting married is that they don't yet have the skills and maturity to have a successful and fulfilling marriage. Then again, many people in their 20s and 30s and even beyond don't know the keys to having a happy, healthy marriage either.

When you believe that any one of the many myths surrounding what makes a good marriage is true, it's enough to keep your marriage from succeeding. Unfortunately, most teenagers believe these myths. They blame each other when they follow what they think are the rules and it ends in misery.

Three major marriage destroying myths are:

1. You can and should meet all each other's needs.
2. You should never disagree or argue with each other.
3. If the relationship is right, you shouldn't have to work at it.

The truth is:

1. You can't meet all of each other's needs. Instead, having a wide circle of friends that includes both men and women will help you feel alive and connected to the world. You just exhaust each other when you expect your partner to like everything you like and want to spend time doing everything you want to do.

2. If you pretend to agree with your partner when you really don't, you won't ever have the chance to learn to negotiate and solve problems together. It's something your spouse does drive you crazy, even if it's something small, it's important to talk about it. If you don't, he'll just be bewildered when you can't stand it anymore and attack him for some other small transgression. You need to learn to talk about the things that bother you.

3. Relationships take an enormous amount of work. Two people who are very different must learn to expose and examine their own beliefs about what's important in their lives. Then they need to find ways to take responsibility for themselves and to help each other manage their lives in an increasingly complex world. Anyone who thinks this should be easy is very naïve.

The reason that most teenagers aren't ready to make a commitment to getting engaged or getting married is that they don't know themselves well enough to manage these complex tasks. One of the main jobs of young adults is to learn about who they are and who they are becoming. My general advice is, learn how to navigate the world on your own before you try to settle down with a life partner and create a successful marriage.

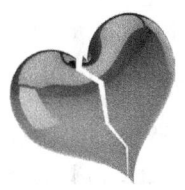

Chapter 8:
How Can You Tell If Your Boyfriend Is Ready to Settle Down And Get Married?

Marianne wants to be married but her boyfriend isn't cooperating. She says:

"We have been together for 5 years, have a 3-year-old and are living together. He said that we are getting married, but I don't know when. Other people say that it's wrong to 'shack up' this way but he's not in a hurry to get married. Should I follow their advice and move out?"

The short answer to Marianne's first question is simple. You observe his behavior. If he asks you to set a date and discuss what kind of wedding you want to have, then he is ready. If he promises that you'll get married eventually, he isn't.

The answer to her second question is more complicated. There are many factors involved and it isn't unusual for couples to delay marriage even though they have children. In fact a New York Times article reported that in the US in 2010, for the first time, over half of babies were born to unmarried women.

The real question for Marianne is "What does 'shacking up' mean to you? Are you both acting like grown-ups, living together and sharing financial responsibility and parenting duties? Or is one of you acting like a kid and expecting the other to be the grown-up? What do you think would change if you did get married?

One of the main things women reported when they were asked what they wished they had known before they married was that their husbands did not change for the better

Are You My Perfect Partner?

after marriage. In fact, negative behavior seemed to get worse. So, if you are imagining that he will 'settle down' if you get married, you are probably going to be disappointed.

Your friends seem to be telling you that your boyfriend has no reason to want to marry you because he is getting all the benefits of being married without any of the responsibilities. Do you think that is the case? If you do, then withdrawing the benefits (at least sex, companionship, spending time with his daughter) might give him a reason to marry you. Or it might give him a good reason to look for someone else to provide the benefits you won't give him. You'll take your chances.

Reading all the secrets women shared in *Being Married: Secrets Women Wish They Knew* will help you decide if getting married to him is a good idea. If it is, I suggest you have a conversation with him that asks him what he will do if you refuse to continue your present arrangement without getting married. He just might tell you. Caution: only have the conversation if you really want to know his answer.

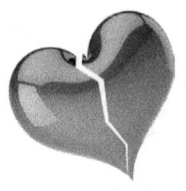

Chapter 9:
At What Age Should I Get Married?

Or, How Very Smart People Make Dumb Relationship Mistakes.

A college student who plans to become a surgeon wonders whether delaying marriage until his 30s, after he has completed his medical education, is a mistake.

He knows that during medical training he'll have little time or energy to put into a marriage. He also knows that he'll be much better prepared to stay connected with a wife and carefully planned children if he waits until then, but he is very worried about missing out on great sex in the meantime.

I think it's great that he's thinking about this now, but he may have an outdated model of what it means to commit to a marriage in the 21st century. He is in danger of looking at the wrong things and creating one more failed marriage.

I am personally prejudiced by the experience of living in a staff housing conclave with many medical residents (doctors in training) and their spouses at a mental hospital where my husband was a staff Psychologist. None of the marriages of my friends who married doctors survived. Mine did—for 58 years and counting.

I have also counseled many other doctors, executives and other very smart people who did and do make these dumb and potentially deadly relationship mistakes.

1. They assume that once you get married the relationship is settled once and for all.
2. They assume that the partner with the lowest status job will sacrifice her (usually) or his (occasionally

and increasingly frequently) individuality to meet the demands of the partner with the higher status job. The partner does not protest that assumption.

3. They equate money and status with happiness.
4. They work extremely long hours to "provide for the family."
5. They decide that the complaints voiced by the lower status partner are unimportant in their greater scheme of things.
6. They ignore requests for joint counseling or participate for 2 or 3 sessions, decide that all the problems are the fault of the lower status spouse and decide that counseling doesn't work.
7. They give lip service to requests to help more or listen more or spend more time with the children. They say they will change, may even change for as long as a month, and then revert to their old behavior.
8. They quickly forget complaints and assume that all is well with the marriage since things seem to be going smoothly.

9. They feel exhausted by their busy schedules and imagine that their spouses simply don't understand the demands of the job. They do not try to explain.
10. They use their busy schedules to excuse their lack of participation in events others consider important.
11. They are shocked when their spouse takes steps to end the marriage.
12. They complain that they had no warning that anything was wrong.
13. They feel devastated and betrayed and blame the lower status spouse.
14. Since they are very smart people, they may come to acknowledge their part in creating the mess.
15. Their spouse may or may not agree to try again—with a new counselor.

I usually get a call at about this stage of the disaster. In some cases, both spouses learn and grow together, salvage the marriage and stay together in a drastically transformed relationship. In other cases, they have been through this cycle often enough that the lower status spouse (traditionally the woman) decides that she has had enough and they divorce—painfully.

This is hard on everyone, especially when children are involved. I believe it's even more important to help prevent such disasters than try to help people recover from them. That's why I write books like this one.

If you are considering marriage with someone like this ambitious student or anyone else, or even if you are already married, learning the secrets women have shared with me and each other will help you avoid this kind of disaster and create a satisfying and fulfilling marriage.

Chapter 10:
Should I Cancel This Wedding?

The wedding is scheduled in four months and Elizabeth asks desperately, "Is there anything I can do to make this work?" Elizabeth and her fiancé have had an on-again off-again relationship for 13 years that started when she was only 15. As the wedding date gets closer his bad behavior has been getting worse.

Elizabeth writes, "He disrespects me, makes jokes about me, puts me down and curses at me when he gets upset. He even kicked a hole in the wall after I got upset because he was cursing at me!" She concludes her appeal for help by saying, "I'm very concerned because we are getting married in four months."

She also writes that she has an appointment with a counselor very soon. That's fortunate because I'm sure her counselor will tell her that no matter how far along the wedding planning has gone and how painful, embarrassing, difficult and potentially expensive it will be to cancel this wedding that's exactly what needs to happen.

Even if her fiancé is behaving badly because he is stressed by the approaching wedding or by Elizabeth's stress about the wedding, he is displaying his anger in extremely immature and dangerous ways. This is an important sign of a potentially abusive relationship. Even if he promises to reform, which appears extremely unlikely, the changes he needs to make before Elizabeth can be safe in his company will take far longer than four months to learn and solidify. And right now, it does not appear that he is even admitting that he has done anything wrong.

Both Elizabeth and her fiancé are minimizing a very serious problem in very different ways. He is denying the existence of a problem at all. He sees nothing wrong in his disrespectful behavior and when she complains about it he blames her and becomes violently angry. If we asked him what he thinks went wrong, he would probably blame Elizabeth for trying to control him.

Elizabeth recognizes that the problem exists but is minimizing the seriousness of the problem. She's looking for a solution that can be implemented within four months so that they can go ahead and get married. She probably knows how unrealistic this is but doesn't want to face the disgrace of admitting to friends and family that she has made a mistake.

Many women that I've worked with and others who shared their secrets to help me prepare my book, *Being Married: Secrets Women Wish They Knew,* have admitted to me that they knew they should never have gone through with their weddings. They knew that something was wrong before the ceremony, but they didn't have the courage to call it off.

These women usually went on to tell me how they did not recognize the signs of an abusive relationship and that the bad behavior got worse after the wedding. Some stayed for many years and some divorced almost immediately. Most implied that if they had known that the consequences of going ahead with the wedding were far worse than they imagined that the consequences of canceling it would have been, they would have told the truth and stopped the wedding.

Elizabeth is facing an important choice point; one that will have lifelong consequences. If she stops the wedding now, she still will have to decide whether to end her engagement. It's possible that her fiancé can learn how to manage his emotions in a healthy and constructive way. He could do this with counseling or with an anger management training program. The shock of Elizabeth setting firm boundaries to protect herself could help him to realize that he has a problem that needs to be addressed. Elizabeth could provide support and encouragement for this change and they could decide to marry in a year or two.

Another possibility is that he can blame Elizabeth for abandoning him by refusing to marry him and not change at all.

Are You My Perfect Partner?

Still another possibility is that they could recognize that things between them have been wrong for a long time and mutually decide to end their engagement. In any case, Elizabeth needs to seriously consider taking care of herself by canceling her wedding plans now.

Hopefully, her family, friends and counselor will help her get through this difficult and challenging part of her life.

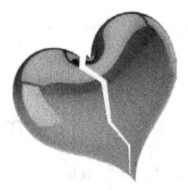

Chapter 11:
Is a 9-Year Age Difference a Problem?

Melissa, a 20-year-old virgin, is concerned about "getting married to a guy who is 9 years older and has more experience in sex life." The wedding is in only 4 months and she is agonizing about not knowing how to please her fiancé sexually. They are clear that they will maintain their sexual boundaries until after they are married but she is ambivalent about letting him know that she has no sexual experience.

She may think that virginity is unusual but recent studies show that over 25 % of 20-year-old women are still virgins.

Are You My Perfect Partner?

Other studies show that the age of first sexual experience is rising among teens.

Of course, a generation or two ago, many women were virgins when they married and definitely anxious about managing their soon to come first sexual experience. Most sought information from friends, magazines, medical professionals and excellent books like *Women's Bodies, Women's Wisdom* by Christiane Northrup, M.D. These resources and many more are still available to Melissa now.

The bigger issue here seems to be one of maturity and resourcefulness. Melissa and her fiancé have apparently never spoken about the potential problems they may encounter—sexual and otherwise. They need to start talking right away. Sometimes pre-marital classes help engaged couples open those discussions.

A 9-year age gap could be a problem for many reasons other than mismatched sexual experience. A 20-year-old has had very limited time to learn about the responsibilities of being an adult in the world. Her interests may be quite different than her husbands. They may both expect her to defer to his judgment because of his greater life experience. He may be ready for children years before she is.

A New York Times article suggests that couples discuss finances, household responsibilities, the desire for children, health concerns and spiritual beliefs among other issues. All of these are important.

Melissa seems to be very naive about marriage and may be a part of a community that supports older men marrying younger women. Matches like this were very common in the past and experienced men expected to initiate their virgin wives sexually. She needs to tell her fiancé about her lack of sexual experience and ask that he be prepared to help her discover what pleases them both. And she needs to start having the conversations that will lay the foundation for a successful and happy marriage.

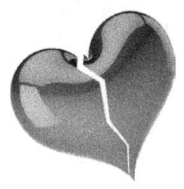

Chapter 12:
My Fiancé loves World of Warcraft

Andrea disapproves of wasting her precious time in a virtual world and wonders whether to seek counseling before getting married. She is afraid that he will become addicted to WoW and start neglecting the real world she cherishes.

She needs to consider three important questions before she makes a decision.

1. What is the connection between passion and addiction?
2. Why is the World of Warcraft game so attractive to her fiancé?

3. Does she want to be in control of how her husband uses his leisure time?

First the connection between passion and addiction is that one can lead to the other. Passion is a term applied to a very strong feeling about a person or thing. Addiction is the continued use of a mood-altering substance or behavior despite adverse consequences. So, it's certainly possible that having a very strong feeling about something, in this case WoW, can be so emotionally involving that it could lead him to want to play so much that he neglects other things in his life.

Second is the question is this likely to happen. That depends on a lot of things. Is World of Warcraft so engaging to her fiancé that he neglects her or working or taking care of himself physically? Or is it a diversion where he gets to hang out with friends (who are not physically present) when he has some leisure time? Does he have other addictive behaviors? Does he smoke? Does he use alcohol excessively? What about drugs? People who do these things often drop one addiction and pick up another.

Are You My Perfect Partner?

The third issue is that Andrea is very adamant that she doesn't like to play World of Warcraft and considers it a waste of her time. A concern is that she is judgmental about anyone playing a virtual game instead of enjoying the "real world" and that she believes that it's virtuous for everyone to avoid that kind of activity. If that's the case, her husband's continuing to play the game would certainly become a problem for her. Then she would undoubtedly try to control his behavior and that would cause friction in their marriage.

Marriages work best when couples learn to balance together time and individual time even though many couples get married with the fantasy that they'll spend all their non-working time together. Exploring both her tendency to be judgmental and his possible addictive tendencies with a counselor would probably be helpful for both Andrea and her fiancé. The counselor will be able to help them decide whether these issues will cause problems after they marry and help them to negotiate what they can do now to avoid those problems.

Chapter 13: My Fiancé Cheated on An Old Girlfriend! Should I Be Getting Married?

Kaileen has been so worried since her fiancé told her that he cheated on another girl several years ago that she has been checking up on his e-mail and wondering whether she should get married. He has told her that he does not intend to cheat on her but that if he does, he'll tell her right away.

It's hard to make a decision like this without listing the pros and cons.

Are You My Perfect Partner?

1. Pro. The fact that he told her about his past before the wedding can be interpreted as being honest with her and trusting her with that information.
2. Con. The fact that she started checking up on his e-mail and found nothing suspicious but is still worried about going through with the marriage implies that she doesn't trust him.
3. Unknown. The fact that he told her he doesn't intend to cheat but implies that he might anyhow it is hard to interpret. It's either a reflection of his honest self-evaluation that he is falible or leaving him an out to cheat again.

I suspect that there's more going on here than Kaileen is admitting or perhaps even aware of. Her intuition may be telling her that something is wrong and she's using his admission of an indiscretion in his past to confirm her uncertainty. She certainly should examine her own feelings of unease that are not related to this incident before deciding whether to ahead with the wedding.

I have encountered many women who have admitted that they got married for the wrong reasons. Some were trying to escape a bad situation. Some were afraid that this was their only chance. Some married because it was expected after a long relationship and engagement. Those women wished that they had had the courage to wait instead of jumping in to a marriage they later regretted.

Kaileen needs to be honest with herself and her fiancé about worries. Learning about what other women have discovered in similar situations may help her clarify some of her concerns. Asking her fiancé what he means when he says he doesn't intend to cheat but he'll tell her right away if he does and letting him know that she's been checking on his e-mail would be a good start.

Premarital counseling would probably be a good idea. Many religious organizations offer classes for engaged couples to help them have the conversations that lay the foundation for a satisfying and lasting marriage.

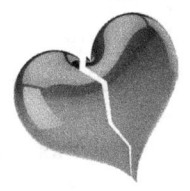

Chapter 14:
My Fiancé Doesn't Stick Up for Me with My Mother-In-Law. Should I Be Getting Married?

Caroline wants to know what to do because her future mother-in-law is extremely controlling, and her fiancé seems to be taking his mother's side in every disagreement. She's worried about marrying him because he has told her that his family will always come first.

Caroline complains that her future mother-in-law acts as if she is in love with her own son, insisting that he spend time with her and devote himself to her needs. She is extremely critical of Caroline both directly and to others in the family.

Her fiancé's ultimatum is that there won't be any wedding unless she builds a stronger relationship with his mother. Why would she want to?

Whether she became involved in this process by agreeing to marry her fiancé before she met his family or whether she knew about his mother's intrusive behavior before she agreed to marry him does not really matter. He has given her plenty of information that he cares more about pleasing his mother than about pleasing or protecting her.

The simple answer is to call off this wedding immediately. Caroline is being treated disrespectfully by her fiancé as well as by his mother. She may hope that this behavior will improve after the wedding, but it is more likely to get worse.

Women who reported what they wish they had known before they married often spoke of being surprised at how much influence their husband's family had on their marriages. They also spoke of wishing they had known that bad behavior tended to get worse.

Unless Caroline calls off the wedding, she is setting herself up for years of abuse and probably a divorce. However, calling off the wedding isn't enough. She also needs to examine her own vulnerability and beliefs that allowed her to get into this situation in the first place.

One more thing women reported is that they wished they had taken the time to get to know themselves better before they married. This is the time for Caroline to do just that to protect herself from getting into a similar situation in the future.

Chapter 15: Is He Really Ready to Commit?

Elena asks if she should be worried because although her boyfriend seems ready to get married now, he was commitment shy until his mid-30s. She wonders if that means there might be some important reason to avoid agreeing to marry him.

It's true that he is marrying a little later than some men but the median age of marriage in the US has been steadily rising since 1960 when it reached an all-time low of 22.8. In 2018 the age was 29.5, which means that half of men do not marry until they are older than that.

Are You My Perfect Partner?

While I don't know a lot about Elena's boyfriend, my guess is that he has not been ready to commit for the same reasons that other men delay marriage. Here are three of the most important reasons.

1. Sex. Back in 1960 it was far harder for a man to have a regular sexual partner unless he married. Now it isn't.
2. Men are afraid of making the wrong choice and getting stuck.
3. Men see marriage as the final step in a long process of growing up.

When sex is readily available men don't see any reason to compromise their freedom by marrying in order to have a ready supply. Both men and women are happy to share sex and live together while they look for permanent partners. They often live together without any expectation that the relationship will last.

Most young adults are searching for the perfect partner. By perfect they mean someone who is willing to accept them as they are without trying to change them. Men also want women who will continue to interest them and not become a boring drag on their lives. They are willing to wait and keep looking around rather than settling for their current companions.

Many men also see their 20s as a time to explore and play as well as to get a strong start in the race to success. They want to keep their responsibilities to a minimum, so they can use most of their resources to meet their own goals. They fear getting tied down to responsibilities too soon and want to wait until the benefits of making a commitment outweigh the potential costs.

So, if Elena is only holding back on agreeing to marry her boyfriend because he has no history of making commitments it would be useful to ask why he has waited so long. If his answers fit into these categories and he meets HER criteria, they have a better than average chance of having a successful marriage. Of course, that does not guarantee that they won't face challenges—they will, and hopefully his maturity will help them meet those challenges.

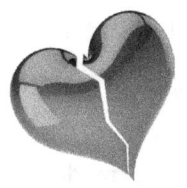

Chapter 16: Are You My Perfect Partner?

This is the guy's side of the commitment quandary.

Matthew, 26, is engaged to be married to Heather. He is completely in love with her but wonders if he should break their engagement because he has not had many relationships and there just might be someone better out there. When he is with her, he is amazingly happy and absolute certain she is perfect for him. When he is away from her, he worries about whether he is making the right decision.

He is struggling with whether to listen to his own inner wisdom—he knows he lights up whenever she is around—

and the cultural myth that insists that the perfect mate (his soul mate?) is waiting for him somewhere and it is his job to find her. He worries that he has not experienced enough women to be certain he has made the right choice.

This is the struggle faced by many young men and women who don't understand three critical relationship realities.

1. There is no such thing as the perfect partner. Soul mates don't exist—only imperfect men and women.
2. Relationships can't magically happen even with this mythical perfect partner. All successful relationships are created through attention and commitment.
3. The wonderful feeling of being totally in love is temporary—sort of like temporary insanity. It is a great way to find a partner, but you need to do much more than just to find her.

Matthew has not shared anything at all about Heather beyond the fact that she is wonderful and that he feels wonderful when he is around her. I must assume that she is a reasonably good match. That means they are from similar cultural backgrounds and are similar in age and have no major health, education or financial challenges to manage.

If Matthew knew about these realities his doubt would probably disappear. He wouldn't consider giving up someone he really enjoys in order to resume his search for the "right one." He would know he and Heather are just at the beginning of learning about each other.

Learning about each other means being together enough that you each see beyond the initial image of perfection to the very real compatibility issues every couple faces.

- What do you each imagine will lead to a rewarding life?
- Does one of you imagine a quiet, private academic life while the other loves excitement, world travel, and bright lights?
- Do you want children?
- Is money and status important?

- Is one an athlete and the other a couch potato?
- How do you like to celebrate holidays?
- When do you like to go to bed and to wake up?
- How do you act when things go wrong as they inevitably do? Do you blame each other or comfort each other or some combination?

Once Matthew learns the answers to these questions, he will have a much better sense of whether he and Heather can build a satisfying marriage together.

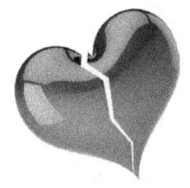

Chapter 17: Afraid to Talk About Getting Married

"I'm afraid to let him know just how much I want to be married to him."

Jessica's boyfriend moved in with her and her three children a year ago because they wanted to be a family. It has worked out beautifully. He's been an excellent father to her three children and she is completely ready to commit to him for the rest of her life. He may be ready to commit to her too. She just isn't sure.

The problem is that both agreed that marriage is just a piece of paper. Now she wants what that piece of paper represents. Jessica writes, "It's the promise to each other that you will do anything to ensure the happiness and well-being of the person you love that I want."

He has hinted about marriage a few times in a joking way. She thinks it's because he wanted to see her reaction and she did her best not to react at all. Jessica is nearly 30 and mature in many ways. She refused to marry the father of her children because she knew that she didn't want to spend her life with him. But when it comes to communicating with her boyfriend about what's very important to her, she sounds like a young teenager. And it sounds as if her otherwise mature boyfriend is in a similar position.

Jessica wants to know how to let him know that she's ready to say yes as soon as he's ready to ask her to marry him. But she's been trying to play things cool for so long that she doesn't know how to do anything else. She clearly does not know how to ask for what she wants.

Are You My Perfect Partner?

Asking risks rejection

Every child is born knowing how to ask for what he or she wants and needs. Babies do it by crying when they need something. Older children ask with words. In fact, most children demand so much it drives their parents to distraction. They know that the worst thing that can happen is that they'll be told "no" and they'll be in the same position they were before they asked. But sometimes, when children ask for what they want they are shamed or hurt and learn that asking is a bad idea. That may have happened to Jessica.

Now Jessica needs to relearn that basic skill. She's not ready to risk rejection by asking the most important question about marriage. So, she needs to start with something smaller. She knows that she's ready to commit to do anything she can to ensure his happiness and well-being. That may be a good place to start. Telling him how happy she is that he is with her before asking him if he feels the same way, when he obviously does, might make her feel safer.

If he sees that Jessica is serious and not being evasive or noncommittal it may make him braver about taking the next step. And if he doesn't, she could continue the conversation, taking just a bit more risk by telling him how much she cares about his happiness and well-being. She could even talk about her changing view about the meaning of that important piece of paper. If he reciprocates by speaking seriously, she can continue the conversation. If he backs away by joking, she can wait and try again another time.

It's scary to start this conversation. What Jessica imagines will happen is probably far worse than what will actually happen.

- One way to manage this fear is to imagine the worst thing that could really happen if she takes the risk of having the conversation.
- Then imagining how she would respond if that did happen will make her feel more in control.

I suspect the answer to that question of what would happen is that she would feel badly. I'm sure she's felt badly before and the feeling passed as feelings do.

Are You My Perfect Partner?

The *7-Day Challenge: Secrets of Reducing Unnecessary Worry*, the gift that comes with this book, is designed to help anyone explore any persistent fears.

Learning to have important, serious conversations is a critical skill she will need in order to have a successful long-lasting marriage.

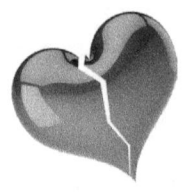

Chapter 18: Will Dad Approve of Her Marriage?

Kate loves her dad, but she is faced with a huge communication challenge because she thinks that he believes that at 26, she is still daddy's little girl. She isn't. She needs to tell him that she plans to get married and she doesn't know how.

After two and a half years of dating, Kate and her boyfriend Jason are ready, both emotionally and financially, to get engaged and set a wedding date. Her mom is finally convinced but her dad has never really considered her boyfriend to be worthy of notice.

Are You My Perfect Partner?

Kate thinks that problem is that her parents are having trouble with her leaving the nest because she is the first child. However, in this family, people apparently need to guess each other's thoughts instead of talking to each other. No wonder she is afraid to talk to her dad.

He isn't used to talking about anything serious with her, so she has never learned to have a conversation with him. She must guess what he is thinking. Up until now she has been a good girl and never challenged him. Now she is imagining that she is really going to upset him, and she doesn't want to.

The truth is that she is making up a story about what her dad is thinking and why her dad has never had a real conversation with his future son-in-law. Kate isn't unusual. In the absence of information, we all make up stories to try to make sense of the world around us.

The problem is not the fact that we make up stories about each other: the problem is that we don't make up enough different stories. Let me explain. We make up one story, believe it, and use it to guide our actions. We rarely wonder whether the story we make up is true, we just assume that it is.

Here is what Kate needs to do:

1. First, she needs to make up more stories—lots of them. She needs to imagine as many different positions her father could take as she possibly can or use these possibilities.

   - He is upset because she wants to leave the nest.
   - He thinks no man is good enough for his daughter.
   - He is shy and has no idea how to talk to any young man she dates.
   - He is secretly wishing for her to leave home, so he can turn her room into his den.
   - He is worried about the current state of the world and wants to protect her.
   - He has been secretly observing Jason and is very happy with her choice.

Are You My Perfect Partner?

- He is expecting her announcement and waiting for it.

2. Next, she should create a few more silly or outlandish things her dad might be thinking and giggle a bit about this list. Hopefully, by now, she will realize that she doesn't really know as much about her dad as she thinks she does.

3. Finally, Kate needs to find a creative way to share the process with him.

    - She could make a Father's Day card that lists all the possibilities and starts with "I wonder what you would think if I told you that Jason and I want to get married." Then list the possibilities: "you would be …" and ask him to check the correct answers.

    - She could just have the conversation starting with "Dad, I think you know how much I love you, but I really don't understand you. I keep making up stories about what I imagine you are thinking. Could you tell me if any of these stories are true?"

- She could act like the grownup she is, recognize that she doesn't really know whether he will be upset and that even if he is, nothing terrible is likely to happen. He will eventually get used to the idea and he will continue to be her dad.
- Kate and Jason could approach her dad together and simply tell him the truth and ask for his blessing.

Doing this conversation planning exercise will help Kate or anyone else prepare for any communication challenge, especially when it involves an important relationship. It will also help Kate learn to have the challenging conversations that every couple faces as they learn to grow and nurture a successful and loving marriage.

Some very useful resources to help manage scary expectations are:

Are You My Perfect Partner?

- The *7-Day Challenge: Secrets of Reducing Unnecessary Worry*, the gift that comes with this book and my popular book,
- *Letting It Go: Relieve Anxiety and Toxic Stress in Just a Few Minutes Using Only Words (Rapid Relief with Logosynthesis.®)*

Chapter 19: Everything Changed: These Newlyweds Are in Trouble!

After living together for four years, they got married a month ago and everything changed! Suddenly Timothy is distant and physically detached. He told Carley that he is uncomfortable with her and doesn't know why. She offered her usual hugs and kisses. Then he asked her for some alone time and to not be so affectionate with him anymore.

Naturally Carley is worried. She asks, "Should I be concerned that getting married has changed how he views me?"

Are You My Perfect Partner?

I can't tell whether marriage has changed Timothy's views of her or of himself, if the reality of being married has overwhelmed him or if getting married has triggered old programming about what married people are supposed to do. I do know that if something isn't done the situation is likely to get worse. I suggest that they make an appointment with a marriage counselor as soon as possible. That's because it's very hard for anyone to unravel this kind of situation by himself or herself.

When I see newlyweds in trouble, I ask each to them to answer these questions while the other is present and listening. They usually can't answer some of them, but every answer helps us to understand the situation.

1. What do you think happened? (Surprisingly they often have a good, if embarrassing, guess.)
2. What did you expect being married to be like?
3. How is it different than what you expected?
4. Is being married different than just living together? How?

5. What was your parents' marriage like from your perspective? (On some level of awareness, you expect your marriage to be like your parents' marriage.)
6. Imagine what a marriage between her mother and his father would be like?
7. Now imagine a marriage between her father and his mother?

By the time the newlyweds have each answered these questions we will all have some good ideas about what is causing the problem. We all carry unconscious ideas about what marriage is supposed to be like based on our experiences when we are small. We decide then what role we will play in our own marriages. Then we forget that we have ever made such a decision.

When we get married the program we created long ago is activated, sometimes to our detriment. By bringing this hidden programming into awareness, it loses some of its power. Thinking consciously about what do want will help you create it.

Are You My Perfect Partner?

My next questions are,

1. Starting from right now, what do you (each) want your marriage to be like?
2. How much of that is in place already?
3. What needs to change to make the rest of the way you want it?
4. How will you start?

Usually the honeymoon stage of your marriage lasts longer than a month or two. Then, the work of growing a marriage together starts. When newlyweds get into trouble early, they need to start the cultivation work a little earlier than usual.

One of the books in this series, *Being Happy Together: What to Do to Keep Love Alive* contains 125 different activities a couple can do together to grow a successful relationship.

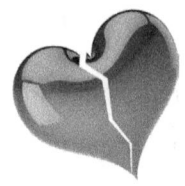

Claim Your Special Bonus Now

For Worriers Who Want to Quit…

Finally: A New, Surprisingly Simple Way to Banish Unnecessary Worry

"Secrets of Reducing Unnecessary Worry: A 7-Day Challenge" Lets You

- Avoid agonizing over what to do
- Escape panic about things that are not likely to happen
- Save yourself from catastrophizing
- ... and much, MUCH More!

The Amazing "Secrets of Reducing Unnecessary Worry: A 7-Day Challenge" Includes:

- 7-Day Challenge
- Daily email reminders
- 5-minute daily action steps

And, I will even revealt the 3 tested magic sentences that dissolve worry.

And best of all, you'll start seeing results in less than 10 minutes a day!

Get started here and use this program to help you with the challenges you face now.

http://www.LaurieWeiss.com/Challenge

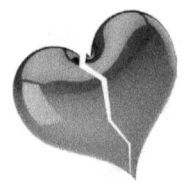

Please Help Me Reach New Readers

Chances are that you checked out the reviews on this book when you purchased it. Reviews are critical to help prospective readers decide to read books. I would be thrilled if you would leave a review NOW, while you are thinking about it.

If you are someone who has done this before, you know how easy it is.

If you're not, you may be shuddering at the memory of grade school book reviews. This is different!!! Really it is!

Are You My Perfect Partner?

All you need to do is imagine that you are telling a friend about reading this book. Then follow these steps.

- Say what you would tell your friend into your phone and record it in the notes section and let your phone write it out. (All you need to say is one or two sentences.)

- Email it to yourself.

- Add punctuation if necessary.

- Cut and paste your sentences into a review box wherever you buy your books.

I have included a few links to popular places to leave your reviews. Go to www.BooksByLaurie.com or www.Goodreads.com/Laurie_Weiss and click on any book title. Scroll down to find the instructions to leave a review.

I would love to hear from you about how this book impacted you. And, if you have any problems or questions about this book, I would really appreciate hearing from you directly. My email address is Laurie@LaurieWeiss.com. You will find my phone number and social media connections on another page.

Thank you in advance for taking the time to contribute to the conversation about what to read. I truly appreciate it.

Laurie

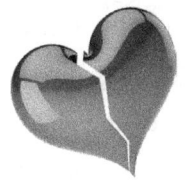

Acknowledgments

This book would not have been possible without the help of many people.

Judith Briles, The Book Sheppard, and my many friends in the Author You community who encouraged me to re-release this book as part of the Secrets of Happy Relationships Series.

Nick Zelinger of NZ Graphics who designed the cover concept and did much more.

Istvan Szabo, Ifj. for both his book formatting skills and his unfailing patience.

Linda Azzi for her Eagle Eye assistance.

And last but certainly not least, my husband and business partner Jonathan B. Weiss for solving my computer problems, for loving me, and for honoring our 58+ year commitment to our own and each other's growth.

Thank you all. I couldn't have done it without you.

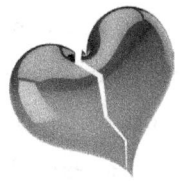

About the Author

Women have been asking Dr. Laurie Weiss questions about relationships for over 45 years. Now she shares her answers to some of them with you.

Relationship Communication Expert, Dr. Laurie Weiss, is internationally known as an expert who helps other relationship consultation professionals develop their skills.

As a psychotherapist, coach, marriage counselor, author and stress-relief expert she has helped more than 60,000 individuals reclaim life energy and find joy in life for more than four decades. She has taught professionals in 13 countries and authored eight books that make complex information accessible to anyone. Her latest, ***Letting It Go***, teaches rapid anxiety and stress relief. http://www.LaurieWeiss.com

Dr. Weiss is one of only two Master Certified Logosynthesis Practitioners in the United States. She is a Certified Transactional Analysis Trainer with Clinical and Organizational Specialties and a Master Certified Coach. Her work has been translated into German, Chinese, Spanish, French and Portuguese.

She is passionate about helping people have the important conversations that build great personal and working relationships. She says, "I have an unshakeable belief, based on over 45 years of experience, that people are doing the very best they can with the resources they have available to them at any given moment."

Dr. Laurie and her husband, Dr. Jonathan B. Weiss, started working together in 1970. Both Drs. Weiss love mixing business and pleasure and enjoy visiting professional colleagues and friends around the globe. They live and work in Littleton, CO, USA.

She loves adventures, went indoor skydiving for the first time at age 67 and zip lining for the first time at age 75. She has been blessed by elephants in India, walked on hot coals, visited Camelot, flown over the Pyramids, and spent an afternoon at the sex temples at Khajiraho and learned more possible sex positions than she can possibly remember.

E-mail: Laurie@LaurieWeiss.com

Office: 303-794-5379

How to Work with Dr. Laurie

My husband, Dr. Jonathan B. Weiss and I have been married since 1960 and business partners since 1972 when we were teaching Transactional Analysis throughout the United States. We have been learning and teaching cutting edge tools for healing and transformation for over 45 years.

We have both been Teaching and Supervising Transactional Analysts for over four decades. Currently we are the only Certified Logosynthesis Practitioners in the United States. Either or both of us would be delighted to help you learn more about creating joy and satisfaction in your life and your important relationships.

Contact Us: We Usually Answer the Phone

You can contact us directly to discuss what is best for you and your group. We offer a variety of options including CLASSES, TALKS, BOOK GROUP VISITS, PROFESSIONAL CONFERENCE PRESENTATIONS, TRAINING, INDIVIDUAL and COUPLES APPOINTMENTS. We work with our clients in person, by phone and by Skype.

Dr. Laurie Weiss:

LaurieWeiss@EmpowermentSystems.com

Dr. Jonathan Weiss: Weiss@EmpowermentSystems.com

Empowerment Systems

506 West Davies Way

Littleton, CO 80120 USA

303-794-5379

Dr. Laurie Weiss

Websites

Personal: http://www.LaurieWeiss.com

Logosynthesis: http://www.LogosynthesisColorado.com

Business: http://www.EmpowermentSystems.com

Purchase Books: http://www.BooksbyLaurie.com

Social Media

Facebook: https://www.Facebook.com/laurieweiss

LinkedIn: http://www.Linkedin.com/in/laurieweiss

Pinterest: https://www.Pinterest.com/laurieweiss/

Twitter: https://Twitter.com/@LaurieWeiss

Goodreads: https://www.Goodreads.com/Laurie_Weiss

ARE YOU MY PERFECT PARTNER?

Blogs

Personal Development:
http://www.IDontNeedTherapy.com/blog

Relationship: http://RelationshipHQ.com/blog/

Business Communication:
http://www.DareToSayIt.com/blog

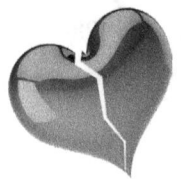

About the Secrets of Happy Relationships Series

Relationships aren't easy. Relationships are often confused and messy with partners trying to find happiness in all the wrong ways.

Real relationships get messy because even though you think your life partner is just like you, he or she isn't. You are two different people trying to meet the challenge of creating and maintaining a happy and loving relationship, perhaps without much useful information.

To make matters worse, you live in the midst of the outmoded role expectations of a culture that values drama and competition and extreme busyness. Most media doesn't help. It focuses on difficult relationships, not successful ones.

Ordinary relationships have their ups and downs and almost nobody writes about those cycles. It's no wonder there are so many misunderstandings. Creating a lasting, loving, growing relationship is an incredible challenge. It's completely natural to have questions about your relationship.

I've been answering questions about relationships since 1973 when I was in newly minted TA (Transactional Analysis) therapist and was sure I had the answers to all the problems of the world. I had been married for 13 years and we had survived some major challenges. I was happily learning and using our new tools. Over four decades later, we are still married, and I've learned a lot.

It's been my pleasure and privilege to help people sort out the misconceptions, misunderstandings and challenges of creating happy, loving relationships. Being happy together is a gift my husband and I have given each other through the work of addressing issues as they arise. It's a gift you can have also; by giving it to each other.

Books in the Secrets of Happy Relationships Series

**Are You My Perfect Partner?
To Marry or Not to Marry …**
Are you really ready to get married?

**Being Married:
Secrets Women Wish They Knew**
*Crucial information you need
to know about marriage*

**Stop Poisoning Your Marriage
with These Common Beliefs**
*Are you letting these myths
undermine your marriage?*

Dr. Laurie Weiss

Relationship Tips for Life Partners
Critical guidelines for creating a true partnership

Reconnect to Rescue Your Marriage:
Avoid Divorce and Feel Loved Again
What to do before leaving your troubled marriage

Stop Arguing and Start Talking …
even if you are afraid your only answer is divorce!
Are you ready to have these loving,
productive conversations with your spouse?

Being Happy Together:
What to Do to Keep Love Alive
Unlock secrets to rapid relationship
renewal in just an hour a week

Other Books by Laurie Weiss

Letting It Go: Relieve Anxiety and Toxic Stress in Just a Few Minutes Using Only Words (Rapid Relief with Logosynthesis®)
Are you ready for relaxation to replace anxiety in your life?

Emotional Self-Help: I Don't Need Therapy, But Where Do I Turn for Answers?
Do you need to become emotionally literate?
www.BooksByLaurie.com/answers

Recovery From CoDependency: It's Never Too Late To Reclaim Your Childhood
Are you ready to release your codependency?
www.BooksByLaurie.com/recovery

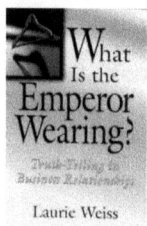

**An Action Plan for Your Inner Child:
Parenting Each Other**
Are you ready to reclaim your inner child?
https://www.amazon.com/dp/1558741658

**What Is the Emperor Wearing?
Truth-Telling in Business Relationships**
Do you wish you dared to tell the truth?
www.BooksByLaurie.com/emperor

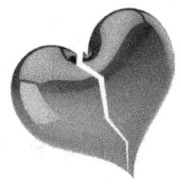

Enjoy this preview of another book in the
Secrets of Happy Relationships series:

Being Married

Chapter 1
What You Should Know, but Don't

*"I wish I'd known what marriage is really like—
instead of swallowing all those myths about marriage."*

Two Don't Become One

When asked what she wished she had known before she got married, Maria answered, "Nothing—I was good to go." When you're young and in love, you too may think you're good to go. You might not be. It depends upon how much you're going to try to make yourself and your marriage measure up to the mythical ideal.

Renee tried! When she started really looking at why she was so unhappy, she realized that she believed it was her job to give up what she loved and embrace what her husband loved in every area of their lives. She just could not live up to her own ideal of what it meant to be a wife.

If you try to constrict yourself into half of who you are in order to become the wife you think you're supposed to be, you may end up surprising yourself by:

- exploding over something simple
- starting to fight frequently about everything and nothing
- getting depressed
- losing interest in making love
- finding someone else so attractive you wonder if you've married the wrong man